# ENDANGERED

## ANIMAL BABIES

Gray Bat

Bald Eagle

Barn Owl

American Burying Beetle

Peregrine Falco

Texas Blind Salamander

Florida Panther

American Alligator

Ocelot

Manatee

Spectacled Bear

Hyacinth Macaw

Blue Whale

Zebra Duiker

Lowland Gorilla

Shoebill Stork

Indian Rhinoceros

Fishing Cat

Reticulated Python

Banded Linsang

Guam Rail

Birdwing Butterfly

Siamang Gibbon

Colobus Monkey

Radiated Tortoise

Tomato Frog

Giant Eland

Bongo Antelope

# ENDANGERED
# ANIMAL
# BABIES

## SAVING SPECIES ONE BIRTH AT A TIME

### BY THANE MAYNARD

A Cincinnati Zoo Book

FRANKLIN WATTS

New York • Chicago • London • Toronto • Sydney

Like mammals everywhere, I was raised by my parents—

Catherine Lobban Maynard
and
Stanley Ansel Maynard

This book is dedicated to them with love and thanks for their laissez-faire parenting style and a long enough leash when I was a boy to let me find my heart in the Florida wilds.

Frontispiece: Polar bears

All photographs copyright © Cincinnati Zoo/Ron Austing except: Cincinnati Zoo/Mike Dulaney: p. 54 bottom; Milan Busching: p. 13; World Wildlife Fund/Ken Balcomb: p. 15; U.S. Fish and Wildlife Service: pp. 23 (R. H. Barett), 35 (Gaylen Rathburn); William Burt: p. 27 top; Zoological Society of San Diego: pp. 29 top (Ron Garrison), 13 (Ken Kelley); Los Angeles Zoo: p. 31 top; Ed Maruska: p. 49 bottom.

Maynard, Thane.
Endangered animal babies : saving species one birth at a time / by Thane Maynard.
p.    cm.—(A Cincinnati Zoo book)
Includes bibliographical references and index.
Summary: Examines such endangered species as the barn owl, birdwing butterfly, and tomato frog and discusses the attempts to save them through captive breeding programs.
ISBN 0-531-11077-X (lib. bdg.).—ISBN 0-531-15257X (trade)
1. Wildlife conservation—Juvenile literature.   2. Endangered species—Breeding—Juvenile literature.   3. Captive wild animals—Breeding—Juvenile literature.   [1. Rare animals—Breeding.
2. Wildlife conservation.]   I. Title.   II. Series.
QL83.M32   1993
639.9—dc20                                              92-33220 CIP AC

# SAVING ANIMAL SPECIES

Every year, as wilderness areas of the world shrink, some animal species are pushed closer to extinction. To save these species from disappearing, zoos are cooperating in a captive breeding program called the Species Survival Plan, or SSP. Through SSP, thousands of animals are sent on breeding loans to zoos and breeding farms around the world. The goal is to increase the populations of the endangered species and to preserve their genetic diversity so that future generations of Siberian tigers, Indian rhinos, reticulated pythons, and other animals will be healthy.

# RAISING ANIMAL BABIES

Animal species have different strategies or methods of raising their young, and their offspring grow up in different ways. Parenting strategies include:

**Eggs**—Most animals—fish, insects, spiders, reptiles, amphibians—hatch from eggs.

**Nursing**—The name mammals comes from the Latin word *mamma*, meaning breast. Mammals nurse their young.

**Intensive care**—Some animals—birds, for example—are fed dozens of times a day when first hatched.

**Offspring on their own**—Many cold-blooded animals, most reptiles, amphibians, fish, and invertebrates, do not feed or protect their young.

**Working fathers**—Among some insects, frogs, and sea horses, males do most of the work of carrying the young or eggs.

**Big baby plan**—Most hoofed mammals, such as zebra and deer, are prey species. Their babies are well developed at birth, so they can run from predators.

**Small baby plan**—Many predator species, such as bears, cats, and wolves, have small offspring as they are less threatened by other animals.

**Many babies**—Fish, opossums, and insects are examples of animals that have many babies at one time, but not all survive.

**One or two at a time**—Most mammals and birds have just a few babies at one time. With fewer offspring needing parental care, a higher percentage of the young survive.

**Unusual births**—Some animals have unique birthing methods. Bats are born upside down; marsupials deliver themselves by crawling up into their mother's pouch.

In the pages that follow twenty-five animals now being bred in captive breeding programs are introduced; with photographs, native range maps, and full descriptions telling how these animals develop and grow and why they need help to survive.

# American Burying Beetle

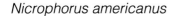

*Nicrophorus americanus*

**Range:** Block Island, eastern Oklahoma
**Habitat:** Diverse habitats, including forests and scrub grasslands
**Reproduction:** Gestation: females lay eggs on buried animal carcass;
eggs hatch in 3 days; larvae transform into beetles after 55–60 days
**Size at Birth:** Grub (larva): 0.25 in. (.64 cm)
**Size of Adult:** 1–2 in long (2.54–5.08 cm); 0.75 (1.92 cm) in wide
**Maturation Period:** 3–4 weeks after pupa stage
**Diet:** Carrion
**Longevity:** 7–12 months
**Threats:** Scarce food supply

American burying beetles live by burying their prey underground. They are a species of carrion beetle, meaning they feed on dead flesh. They perform the essential role of scavengers; they feed on the bodies of dead animals and so dispose of them.

After a small animal's death, these insects rush in and dig away the soil to bury it. The female then lays eggs on the dead animal's carcass, which will then provide the beetle larvae with food when they hatch.

Burying beetles bury their prey in order to keep competitors—such as flies—away from it. Flies also lay eggs on dead animals and their eggs hatch in just a few hours. The tiny maggots which emerge would beat beetle larvae to the feast.

Burying beetles are remarkable diggers, capable of burying a blue jay in less than a minute. The beetles are capable fliers and sometimes fly to the carcass to begin burying it. Scientists also believe the beetles may be signaled when and where to dig by the pressure of the dead animal lying on the soil above them. Insects smell with their antennae, and those on a burying beetle are large and sensitive enough to enable it to sense a dead animal through 2 feet (.61 m) of soil or from a great distance above ground.

At one time this species lived in 42 states, but today burying beetles live only on Block Island, off Rhode Island, and in a single county in eastern Oklahoma. Scientists are not certain why only two populations remain, but feel it is valuable to find out why. They may be an indicator of the health of our environment.

# Bald Eagle

*Haliaeetus leucocephalus*

**Range:** Alaska, Florida, western Canada; sparse distribution in North America

**Habitat:** Roost in forest trees near streams or open water

**Reproduction:** Gestation: 31–46 day incubation clutch of 2 eggs (occasionally 1 or 3) per season

**Size at Birth:** Egg 3–4 in long (7.62–10.16 cm), weighing 3–5 oz (85.05–141.75 g)

**Size of Adult:** 7–14 lbs (3.18–6.35 kg); 30–36 in long (76.20–91.44 cm); 6.5–7 ft (1.98–2.13 m) wingspan

**Maturation Period:** 4 years

**Diet:** Fish; less often rabbits, squirrels, waterfowl

**Longevity:** 25–30 years

**Threats:** Pollution (pesticides); human encroachment

Bald eagles are famous as the symbol of the United States. They could be noted, too, for their care for their young.

Bald eagles build the largest nests in the world. These stick-and-foliage structures can be 9 feet (2.74 m) around, and 12 feet (3.66 m) deep. The nests are added to year after year and can weigh more than a ton (907.20 kg). They may be built 70 feet (21.34 m) above the ground, in a treetop or on a cliff near the water.

Although eagles are thought to pair for life, each year they go through a courtship ritual that includes high-speed swoops, dives, and somersaults. Often the pair will mate in midair.

Females typically lay a clutch of 2 eggs, which the parents incubate in turns until they hatch. In the first 3 months of the eaglets' lives, the parents feed them and teach them to fly and to catch fish and other prey. Then the adults chase the young from their territory, forcing them to find their own. This may seem harsh, but eagles need a large prey base and territory.

Bald eagles appear to be making a comeback. In 1986 there were no nesting pairs in Tennessee, but in 1990, 11 nests were seen. In Ohio there were 6 eagle nests in 1980, and 17 in 1992. The Cincinnati Zoo has helped the eagle. Between 1982 and 1992, the zoo placed 5 captive-bred eaglets in nests near Lake Erie, and a pair of eaglets in Tennessee.

The bald eagle is not out of danger. Only some nests have young. To help this bird, we must reduce air and water pollution and the use of dangerous pesticides.

# Banded Linsang

*Prionodon linsang*

**Range:** W. Malaysia, Sumatra, Java, Borneo
**Habitat:** Tropical rain forest and undergrowth
**Reproduction:** Gestation: 45–60 days; 1–3 (usually 2)
offspring per litter per 6 months
**Size at Birth:** 2–4 oz (56.70–113.40 g); 6 in long
(15.24 cm) including tail
**Size of Adult:** 1.5 lbs (.68 kg); 2.5 ft long (.75 m)
(nearly half is the tail)
**Maturation Period:** Male: 2 years; Female: 1 year
**Diet:** Squirrels, spiny rats, birds, crested lizards, and insects
**Longevity:** About 8 years in captivity; unknown in wild
**Threats:** Habitat loss due to human encroachment;
Agent Orange poisoning during Vietnam War

The banded linsang, a resident of the Southeast Asian rain forests, is named for the pattern on its catlike fur. It is an elusive animal; one of the rarest and least known of the civets, a group of mammals related to the mongoose. The linsang is the most cat-like of all the civets, and it may resemble the extinct ancestor of all cats—from house cats to tigers. One catlike characteristic is its retractile claws.

Linsangs lead solitary lives. Young females stay with their mothers until they are mature at about a year, but males are on their own soon after they are weaned at about 2 months. Baby linsangs, like baby cats, are small and defenseless at birth.

Linsangs are arboreal (tree dwelling) and nocturnal (active at night). They sleep during the day in leaf-and-stick-lined nests up in trees or under roots or logs, emerging to hunt through the trees at night.

Linsangs are long and slender, with short legs and long noses, and are well adapted for hunting in trees. And what hunters they are! Their prey—squirrels, rats, birds, and lizards—are all fast and alert, so how do linsangs catch them? Long tails serve these graceful animals as balancing poles. They move almost like snakes—speeding along branches or the ground—then wait in ambush, using camouflage and speed to catch their dinner, which they polish off with their sharp incisors and long canines.

# Barn Owl

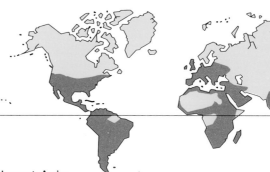

*Tyto alba*

**Range:** Europe, United States, Africa, Southeast Asia, and Australia

**Habitat:** Buildings (barns, church steeples, water towers, dilapidated buildings), hollow trees, caves, and other secluded places

**Reproduction:** Gestation: 32–34 day incubation; 4–7 eggs per clutch every 6 months

**Size at Birth:** Eggs 1.5–2.5 in long (3.82–6.36 cm), weighing .5–1 oz (14.18–28.35 g)

**Size of Adult:** 0.5–1 lb (0.23–0.45 kg); 11–17 in (27.94–43.18 cm) long from head to tail

**Maturation Period:** 1–3 years

**Diet:** Small rodents

**Longevity:** 10–17 years

**Threats:** Habitat destruction, resulting in loss of prey base

Barn owls get their name from their habit of nesting in barns and other buildings. Baby barn owls are featherless upon hatching. They develop a covering of fluffy white down in their first two weeks, then start to grow feathers and develop the appearance of their parents. Both parents feed and care for their young.

Barn owls inhabit all of the continents except Antarctica. Although widespread, barn owls are not common in most of their range. In North America and the British Isles they are endangered species.

Other owls, such as the barred owl and great horned owl, have healthy populations in North America. But the barn owl is a specialist; it feeds on small rodents such as meadow voles and white-footed mice. The prey is found only in open undisturbed areas, and in what farmers call "old fields," areas that haven't been plowed for a few years. Today, with intensive agricultural methods, fall plowing, and no land left fallow, barn owls are running out of places to hunt.

Although barn owls breed well in captivity, they could starve when released into the wild. Barn owls can't just adapt and start to eat food that is available because their size limits the kinds of prey they can kill. Barn owls stand over 1 foot high (.30 m), but most of their bulk consists of feathers, and they weigh only about half a pound (.23 kg). Therefore, they are not capable of killing mammals as large as rabbits or rats.

# Birdwing Butterfly

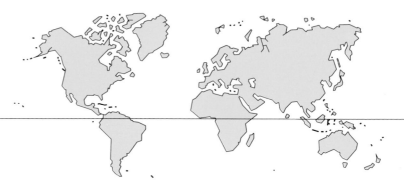

*Ornithoptera priamus*

**Range:** New Guinea
**Habitat:** Rain forest
**Reproduction:** Gestation: female lays eggs on leaves of
Aristolochia plant (tropical vine); eggs hatch in 1 week;
caterpillar (larva) eats leaves and in 5 weeks pupates;
pupa emerges as adult butterfly in 2 weeks
**Size at Birth:** Caterpillar is less than 1 oz (0.25 g) and 0.25 in (.64 cm) long
**Size of Adult:** Butterfly has a 6–10 in (15.24–25.40 cm) wingspan
**Maturation Period:** 1 month
**Diet:** Flower nectar
**Longevity:** 4–6 weeks
**Threats:** Habitat destruction

The birdwings are the stars of the butterfly world. With wingspans of up to 10 inches (25.40 cm), they are the largest of all butterflies. Their colors are spectacular! Males range from yellow to green or bright blue, and females, with better camouflage, are often brown with lighter spots.

Like all butterflies and moths, the birdwing butterfly undergoes complete *metamorphosis* on its way to becoming an adult. It hatches from a tiny egg; is a caterpillar during its larval stage, eating lots of leaves in order to grow. The caterpillar pupates, enclosed in a chrysalis, which is a protective coating like a moth's cocoon. After a period of weeks, an adult butterfly emerges from the pupa and begins the whole process again by searching for a mate.

The people of the island country of Papua New Guinea have found a unique way to help birdwing butterflies. Ranchers plant gardens with the butterflies' favorite flowers. The butterflies are attracted to the gardens and lay eggs there. Ranchers collect the butterfly pupae and raise them to adults. Some adults are released to replenish the world's butterfly populations; the rest are sold to collectors. Both the people and animals profit: the people earn money and become involved in local conservation, and the butterflies receive protection. Other countries are beginning butterfly ranching programs also.

# Blue Whale

*Balaenoptera musculus*

**Range:** Arctic and Antarctic regions in summer; subtropical latitudes in winter
**Habitat:** Deep ocean waters
**Reproduction:** Gestation: 11 months; 1 offspring every 2 years
**Size at Birth:** 2,500 lbs (1,134 kg); 25 ft (7.62 m) long
**Size of Adult:** 100–135 tons (90,720–122,472 kg); 85–100 ft (25.91–30.48 m) long
**Maturation Period:** 5 years
**Diet:** Plankton, shrimplike food (especially krill in the Antarctic)
**Longevity:** 80 years
**Threats:** Poaching for blubber

Without doubt, the biggest baby in the world is a baby blue whale. This isn't surprising since the blue whale is the largest creature ever to roam the Earth.

Blue whales are also the fastest growing animals on Earth. From conception to birth, just 11 months, the fetus of this mammal whale grows from the size of a speck of dust to 25 feet (7.62 m) in length and over 2,500 pounds (1,134 kg) in weight. Mother whales generally give birth in winter, in the warmer waters near the equator, which they use as calving areas. Whales do not have a well-developed insulating layer of blubber at birth, so they must eat a great deal to build up reserves before they swim with their mothers to the colder Arctic or Antarctic waters. They drink as much as 150 gallons (567.78 l) a day of their mother's milk during their 8 nursing months, and can gain 200 pounds (90.72 kg) in a single day. On its first birthday, a blue whale can be ten times its birth size, and weigh 25,000 pounds (11,340 kg)! By the time the baby is weaned, the whales have reached polar waters where krill, the blue whale's principal food source, is plentiful.

Because of the long gestation and nursing periods, female blue whales usually have only 1 calf at a time, every 2 years at the most. Female blue whales are larger than the males.

Unfortunately, despite more than two decades of bans on whaling, the world population of blue whales is thought to be fewer than 1,000 animals.

# Bongo Antelope

*Tragelaphus eurycerus*

**Range:** Eastern, central and western Africa
**Habitat:** Lowland forest
**Reproduction:** Gestation: 9.5 months; 1 offspring per 10-month period
**Size at Birth:** 40–50 lbs (18.14–22.68 kg)
**Size of Adult:** Male: 700–800 lbs (317.52–362.88 kg);
Female: 400–450 lbs (181.44–204.12 kg)
**Maturation Period:** 2–2.5 years
**Diet:** Primarily grasses
**Longevity:** 17 years
**Threats:** Habitat loss; poaching

The bongo antelope is one of the most beautiful hoofed mammals in Africa. Unfortunately, due to a growing human population, poaching, and habitat loss, bongos are fast becoming an endangered species and are threatened throughout much of their range.

Baby bongos are born with the same richly colored coats—rust with thin, white vertical stripes—as their parents, but they don't yet have horns. These will grow up to 30 inches (76.20 cm) long during the first few years of the bongo's life. The most notable feature of a baby bongo is the ears, which are proportionally much larger than the adult's.

Bongos have been born at the Cincinnati Zoo through *embryo transfer*. A fertilized egg (embryo) of one animal is placed into another female to develop. Bongos normally only have 1 baby per year, but with the use of fertility drugs, females can produce more eggs. Scientists then transfer embryos into other female animals to develop, to increase the numbers of this endangered antelope.

In 1984, the Cincinnati Zoo's C.R.E.W. (Center for Reproduction of Endangered Wildlife) team performed the world's first successful interspecies embryo transfer. The embryo of a bongo antelope was placed into a female of a different species, a common eland antelope. The common eland is not endangered, and there are many in captivity. Thus scientists will have future opportunities for embryo transfers.

Today, scientists can freeze embryos from endangered species in a "frozen zoo" for future use. Bongo embryos, and others, are frozen in tanks of liquid nitrogen to serve as an icy insurance policy for vanishing species.

# Colobus Monkey

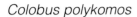

*Colobus polykomos*

**Range:** East and central Africa
**Habitat:** Dense forest
**Reproduction:** Gestation: 165 days; 1 offspring per year
**Size at Birth:** 0.9 lb (0.41 kg); 8 in (20.32 cm) total body length
**Size of Adult:** 1.5–2.5 ft (.46–.76 m) in head-body length
with a tail of 2–2.5 ft (.61–.76 m)
**Maturation Period:** 5 years
**Diet:** Primarily leaves, seeds, and shoots
**Longevity:** 20 years
**Threats:** Habitat loss due to farming

At birth a colobus monkey weighs less than a pound (0.45 kg) and is covered with white hair, making it easy to spot in a group of black-and-white adult monkeys. Different females in the group sometimes carry a young colobus, but after just a couple of weeks, this mammal baby is strong enough to cling to its mother's fur as the adult climbs through the trees foraging for leaves. At 6 weeks a young colobus begins to eat leaves, but it is not fully weaned until it is about 7 months old.

Colobus monkeys typically live in large family groups of 20 or more, and this group life provides safety for the colobus. Eagles and human beings are among their few predators, although Jane Goodall, who studied chimpanzee behavior in Africa for 30 years, did witness adult chimps killing and eating a colobus.

The black and white colobus of east Africa is the most dramatic looking of the three colobus species. Its long, shaggy white tail and black and white markings make the skins sought after for capes and headdresses for traditional African ceremonies. The added pressure of commercial fashion nearly caused the extinction of the colobus when this fur became the rage in nineteenth-century Europe. It was estimated that by 1892, almost 200,000 colobus skins had been exported to the European market. Even today, rugs and wall hangings made of the distinctive tails of the colobus monkey can be seen for sale in African shops and villages. Fortunately, international laws prohibit the import of these items into most nations.

# Fishing Cat

*Felis viverrina*

**Range:** Sumatra, Java, to South China and India,
Ceylon, Thailand
**Habitat:** Forests, swamps, and marshy areas
**Reproduction:** Gestation: 63 days; 1–4 offspring per
litter; 1–2 litters per year
**Size at Birth:** Less than 0.5 lb (0.23 kg);
3–4 in (7.62–10.16 cm) head-body length
**Size of Adult:** 12–18 lbs (5.45–8.17 kg); 3 ft (.91 m) head-body length
**Maturation Period:** 1–1.5 years
**Diet:** Fish, small mammals, birds, insects, crustacea
**Longevity:** 10–13 years
**Threats:** Human encroachment, habitat loss

Most people believe that cats hate the water, perhaps because house cats are only exposed to bathtubs and garden hoses. However, some wild cats love to swim, including the tiger and the fishing cat. As the name implies, fishing cats of Indonesia, South China, and India are skilled at catching fish in rivers and streams. Fishing cats are able to catch fish while completely immersed in the water, or by reaching into the water from shore. Their paws are slightly webbed to aid movement in the water. They are nocturnal animals and often catch fish by looking for their reflection in the moonlight. Fish are not their only prey; they also eat small mammals, birds, insects, and aquatic invertebrates such as crayfish.

Fishing cat littermates play and chase one another near the water, learning skills they will need to survive as aquatic predators. Fishing cat babies are weaned from their mother at about 4 months. As adults, they are medium-sized wild cats.

Fishing cats are well camouflaged for life in low country forests and swamps. Their short, coarse fur is spotted with black markings on a gray and light brown coat. But even the best disguise won't protect them from encroaching agriculture and forestry projects throughout their native habitat. Like wild cats everywhere, fishing cats need remote areas in order to survive.

# Guam Rail

*Rallus owstoni*

**Range:** Native to Guam, now extinct in the wild
**Habitat:** All habitats except wetlands
**Reproduction:** Gestation: 30–35 days incubation;
2–4 eggs per clutch
**Size at Birth:** 0.5 oz (14.18 g)
**Size of Adult:** 0.5 lbs (0.23 kg); 1 ft (.30 m) long
**Maturation Period:** 6 months
**Diet:** Slugs, snails, insects, amphibians, flowers, and seeds
**Longevity:** Unknown in the wild, up to 5 years in captivity
**Threats:** Extinction due to the accidental introduction of
the brown tree snake from New Guinea and coastal Australia.

The Guam Rail once was found only on the island of Guam. Today it is not found even there! The Guam Rail is extinct in the wild, and the only homes these birds now have are in zoos. If the captive breeding programs in progress are successful, we may once again see this bird fly free.

It is believed that in the 1940s, a venomous snake called the brown tree snake was accidently introduced to the island of Guam. Unfortunately, as its name implies, the brown tree snake lives and hunts in trees, specializing in birds as its prey. And since Guam previously had no predators like this, the birds had no natural defenses. As a result, 5 species of birds living on the island of Guam became endangered. Three of those species are now extinct. An effort is underway to help the remaining two, the Guam Rail and the Micronesian Kingfisher, make a comeback.

Through captive breeding programs in progress since 1984, the Guam Rail is now being established in the wild. On February 1, 1990, 30 birds were released onto the island of Rota, off the coast of Guam. The island is very similar in habitat to the bird's native home, and there are no brown tree snakes there. Scientists hope that this bird will be successful in the wild, and that the Micronesian Kingfisher will be the next bird to find a new home on the island of Rota.

# Hyacinth Macaw

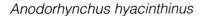

*Anodorhynchus hyacinthinus*

**Range:** East-central South America
**Habitat:** Swamps, forests, and palm groves
**Reproduction:** Gestation: 25–35 day incubation
**Size at Birth:** 1–2.5 in (2.54–6.36 cm) long
**Size of Adult:** 35 in (88.90 cm) long
**Maturation Period:** 2–4 years
**Diet:** Seeds, nuts, fruits
**Longevity:** 30–80 years
**Threats:** Pet trade and tropical forest destruction

The hyacinth macaw, the largest of all parrots, is native to the Brazilian tropical rain forests south of the Amazon River. These cobalt blue birds are magnificent in flight, often traveling in pairs and sometimes in groups of more than a dozen.

Like nearly all 327 species of parrots, the hyacinth macaw eats fruits, seeds, and nuts, which its oversized bill is well adapted for opening. And, like other macaws, the hyacinth macaw makes its nest in the hollow of a tree, which provides protection from predators. Hyacinth macaws prefer to nest inside palm trees, something that was only recently learned at zoos. Today many zoos hang sections of palm-tree trunks in their macaw cages to encourage nest building.

Newly hatched macaws are featherless, awkward-looking creatures whose parents feed them partially digested fruits and seeds. If hand-reared in a zoo, a youngster gets similar food, most often through a plastic syringe.

Parrots, including macaws, are popular as pets. But there are a few things to consider before buying one. Parrots are among the noisiest animals, and often call loudest in the early morning. Parrots can be destructive. With their beaks they can tear up furniture, and a macaw's beak is strong enough to bite off a finger. Some parrots live 50 or 60 years, so buying one as a pet may be a lifetime commitment. Many popular pet species are endangered in the wild, so be **certain** that your parrot was hatched in captivity before you buy it.

# Indian Rhinoceros

*Rhinoceros unicornis*

**Range:** Nepal, India, Southwest Asia
**Habitat:** Open areas, marshes, swamp land
**Reproduction:** Gestation: 16 months; 1 offspring every 3–5 years
**Size at Birth:** 90–120 lbs (40.82–54.43 kg)
**Size of Adult:** Male: 2.5 tons (2,268 kg); Female: 1–1.5 tons (907.2–1,360.8 kg); up to 6 ft 4 in (1.95 m) high at the shoulder
**Maturation Period:** Male: 5–6 years; Female: 5 years
**Diet:** Primarily grasses
**Longevity:** 35–45 years
**Threats:** Poaching; habitat loss due to farming

Sometimes called the "one-horned rhino," the Indian rhinoceros is more easily identified by its deeply folded skin, which looks like heavy armor. At birth, Indian rhinos stand about 2 feet (.61 m) high and weigh about 90–120 pounds (40.82–54.43 kg). They can eventually reach over 6 feet (1.83 m) in height at the shoulder and a weight of 5,000 pounds (2,268 kg).

Like all mammals, rhinos nurse from their mothers. Young rhinos are prey for tigers and stick close to their mother's side for over a year. This, combined with the 16-month gestation, explains why Indian rhinos have at the most, 1 calf every 3 years.

Indian rhinos are active by day, grazing on short grasses and water plants. Like all species of rhinos, they often frequent wallowing holes. In dry seasons, these scarce holes may be shared by a dozen rhinos, all soaking themselves in water and mud. At night, Indian rhinos often sleep in "tunnels" they create in the 12- to 27-foot-high (3.66–8.23 m) elephant grass. Unlike their African cousins, Indian rhinos have scent glands on their front feet that secrete a substance used for marking their territories. They also leave a trail of droppings to mark their areas.

The Indian rhinoceros once had a broad range that reached from northern India to Nepal and Bhutan. Today this endangered species is restricted to ever-shrinking habitats in protected reserves in Nepal, India, and southwest Asia. Human population growth has caused wholesale habitat destruction, which, combined with poaching for their horns, is reducing the numbers of Indian rhinos.

# Lowland Gorilla

*Gorilla gorilla*

**Range:** Cameroon, Central African Republic, Gabon, Congo, and equatorial Guinea
**Habitat:** Jungles of western Africa
**Reproduction:** Gestation: 250–270 days; 1 offspring every 3–4 years
**Size at Birth:** 3–5 lbs (1.36–2.27 kg)
**Size of Adult:** Male: 310–450 lbs (140.62–204.12 kg), 5.6–6 ft (1.71–1.82 m) tall; Female: 200 lbs (90.72 kg) or less, 5 ft (1.52 m) tall
**Maturation Period:** Male: 8–9 years; Female: 6–7 years
**Diet:** Herbs, shrubs, vines
**Longevity:** 35 years in the wild, 50 years in captivity
**Threats:** Human encroachment, poaching, habitat loss

Gorillas are the largest primates in the world. Human beings are the second biggest. And like us, gorillas take quite a while to mature. Babies generally weigh from 3–5 pounds (1.36–2.27 kg) at birth and take 6 or 7 years to mature to the point where they can have their own young. Baby gorillas nurse until 2 years of age, and by then eat solid foods.

Gorillas are very social animals; they live in large family groups with 5 to 10 females and their offspring as well as a dominant adult male. The youngsters learn how to be parents through the interaction of the family group, which is called a "troop." For this reason, zoos try to leave baby gorillas with their mothers. This is not just so they can nurse and drink their mother's milk with all the important nutrients and antibodies it contains, but also because gorillas have a lot to learn as they mature. They need to know how to forage for food in the rain forest, how to fend for themselves, and how to escape predators. For a wild animal species, the gorilla takes a long time to grow up—not quite as long as people, but about 6 years.

The primary threats to gorillas are deforestation and poaching. Recently, though, gorillas have started to become a success story. Gorillas have been drawing tourists from around the world to Africa, providing income for local people. Unfortunately, political instability and civil war in the countries where gorillas live can put an end to both the tourist trade and the gorillas.

# Manatee

*Trichechus manatus*

**Range:** Caribbean from the southeastern United States to northern South America
**Habitat:** Coastal lagoons, estuaries, freshwater rivers
**Reproduction:** Gestation: 150–180 days; 1 calf every 2–3 years
**Size at Birth:** 45 lbs (20.41 kg); 3.5 ft (1.07 m) long
**Size of Adult:** Up to 3,500 lbs (1,587.60 kg); 12–15 ft (3.66–4.57 m) head-tail length
**Maturation Period:** 5–8 years
**Diet:** Floating or submerged sea grasses (especially eelgrass) and other aquatic plants
**Longevity:** Up to 50 years in the wild
**Threats:** Poaching for flesh and hides; habitat destruction due to increasing use of outboard motor boats

Manatees are huge, slow-moving aquatic mammals. In fact, manatees are one of the biggest animals in North America. At 12 feet (3.66 m) in length and weighing 3,500 pounds (1,587.60 kg), they need 100 pounds (45.36 kg) of water plants every day.

A female manatee is fertile for only a 2-week period every year, during which time it mates with several males. After a 5- to 6-month gestation, a single calf is born, weighing about 45 pounds (20.41 kg). The calf nurses underwater for several months. Nursing from their mothers is a characteristic common to all mammals. Manatees have young only every 2 to 3 years. The species has no apparent social structure, but congregates, especially in winter, in herds numbering in the hundreds. If undisturbed, manatees live about 50 years.

The manatee is often called the Florida manatee since it lives in rivers in that state. The species is also known as the West Indian manatee because it ranges through the Caribbean and in northern rivers in South America. Although the manatee is a protected species, it is still endangered due to poaching and to powerboat accidents in the United States. There are nearly half a million boats in Florida, and these slow swimmers can't get out of the way. Many adult manatees sport deep scars from boat propellers and, tragically, many have died.

People are trying to help manatees. Researchers using radio telemetry and aerial photography are investigating their behavior and habitat needs. The efforts seem productive and the manatee population has grown slowly in the last 20 years.

# Ocelot

*Felis pardalis*

**Range:** Southwest United States, Mexico, Central America, and South America north of Paraguay
**Habitat:** Forest and steppe
**Reproduction:** Gestation: 70 days; 2–4 kittens per litter per year
**Size at Birth:** 8 oz (226.80 g); 4 in (10.16 cm) long
**Size of Adult:** 25–35 lbs (11.34–15.88 kg); up to 4 ft (1.22 m) long with 15 in (38.10 cm) tail
**Maturation Period:** 1–1.5 years
**Diet:** Small mammals, birds, and reptiles
**Longevity:** 10–13 years
**Threats:** Poaching for the fur trade

The ocelot is a beautiful, medium-sized cat whose name is derived from the Mexican word *tlalocelotl*, meaning "field tiger." As the name suggests, ocelots do not live only in the rain forests of Central and South America, but range from the Amazon valley north to Mexico and even, though rarely, the southwest United States.

Breeding may occur at various times of the year, not just in one season. A gestation of 70 days results in a litter of 2 to 4 kittens that are born blind, but well-furred, in a nest in a hollow log, a cave, or dense vegetation. This is one reason you often see nest boxes in zoo cat exhibits. Field biologists have monitored the breeding behavior of cats in the wild, and suggested that zoos wanting a successful breeding program provide "denning boxes" in which females can bear their young.

Ocelots have been made into fur coats or pets. Neither is a great idea. It takes from 20 to 40 ocelot skins to make a single coat, and although young ocelots can be playful and cute, once they reach maturity they change and become dangerous. Fortunately, ocelots and other endangered species are protected from illegal trade by a program called the Convention of International Trade of Endangered Species, or CITES. Under the CITES agreement, it is illegal to bring any endangered species, or products made from one, into the United States. As a result, whether it's a coat or a pet, if it has ocelot fur, you can't buy it.

# Peregrine Falcon

*Falco peregrinus*

**Range:** All continents (except Antarctica) and many oceanic islands

**Habitat:** Clefts, ledges, potholes, rocky cliffs, tall buildings, occasionally trees, and sometimes sandy ground (in tundra and on islands)

**Reproduction:** Gestation: 28–29 day incubation; 3–4 eggs per clutch per year

**Size at Birth:** 5–7 oz (141.75–198.45 g) at 10 days

**Size of Adult:** less than 2 lbs (.91 kg); 15–19 in (38.10–48.26 cm) long; 43–46 in (109.22–116.84 cm) wingspan; female larger than male

**Maturation Period:** 2–3 years

**Diet:** Birds and rodents

**Longevity:** 10–15 years

**Threats:** Pollution (pesticides)

The peregrine falcon is making a comeback! As recently as the 1970s, the North American population of this species was extinct east of the Mississippi River. The pesticide DDT reduced the peregrine's ability to produce calcium, resulting in the thinning of the shells of their eggs. The parent birds then sometimes crushed the eggs, accidently killing their offspring. Today, eliminating DDT from the environment and intensive captive breeding have helped the peregrine recover.

Baby falcons are defenseless. They hatch out featherless, with their eyes not yet open, and require nearly constant attention for a few weeks. As with all birds of prey, both parents care for the young, hunting birds on the wing to keep their brood fed and growing. Peregrines first fly and hunt on their own at about 7 weeks of age.

In the 1960s, a team of scientists led by Dr. Tom Cade of the Cornell University Ornithology Lab established The Peregrine Fund and began to breed peregrine falcons in captivity and release the offspring in the wild. Their efforts helped increase the falcon population and raised people's awareness of the plight of this bird.

Downtown skyscrapers are one of the places baby falcons have been successfully released. Naturally nesting on high rocky cliffs, the peregrines have taken very easily to these new roosts and are now breeding on their own in many cities across the United States.

# Reticulated Python

*Python reticulatus*

**Range:** Southeastern Asia and nearby Pacific islands
**Habitat:** Dry jungle
**Reproduction:** Gestation: Female lays eggs 3–4 months
after mating and incubates eggs for 2–3 months; up to
100 eggs per clutch per year
**Size at Birth:** 2–2.5 ft (.61–.76 m) long
**Size of Adult:** 32 ft (9.75 m) long
**Maturation Period:** About 2 years; varies because maturity
is determined primarily by rate of growth rather than age
**Diet:** Mammals and birds, occasionally snakes and large lizards
**Longevity:** 28 years
**Threats:** Leather trade, habitat loss

Pythons are *oviparous*, meaning they lay eggs, as do most other snakes. Reptile species in which the female holds the eggs inside its body while they develop and then gives birth to live young are called *viviparous*. Viviparous snakes include rattlesnakes, garter snakes, and boas.

Most snake eggs are soft and leathery compared to the hard-shelled eggs of birds. When the young pythons first hatch, they are about 18 inches (45.72 cm) long and capable of eating a mouse for their very first meal.

The name "reticulated" refers to the elaborate pattern on the skin of the snake. Reticulated pythons grow to be the biggest snakes in the world, sometimes reaching 32 feet (9.75 m) in length and weighing over 500 pounds (226.80 kg). They start life in an egg 2 to 3 inches (5.08–7.62 cm) in length which the mother incubates. This may not sound unusual, since almost all of the 9,000 species of birds sit on their eggs. But reptiles are cold-blooded and generally cannot warm their eggs. Female reticulated pythons curl their bodies around their clutch of eggs, covering them, which helps stabilize the temperature. "Sitting" on the eggs would smash them.

Most amazing though, is the python's ability to raise its body temperature through a series of muscle contractions that make the animal appear to have hiccups. Scientists know that this body movement can raise the mother's temperature 3 degrees, but no one is certain why pythons perform this unusual incubation while most snakes do not.

# Shoebill Stork

*Balaeniceps rex*

**Range:** Southern Sudan and central Africa
**Habitat:** Papyrus and reed swamps
**Reproduction:** Gestation: 45 days incubation; 2 eggs per clutch per season
**Size at Birth:** Unknown to date
**Size of Adult:** 11–13 lbs (4.99–5.90 kg); 40 inches (101.60 cm) high
**Maturation Period:** One year
**Diet:** Fish (especially lungfish), baby crocodiles, water snakes, and occasionally small turtles
**Longevity:** Unknown for certain, expected to be up to 15 years
**Threats:** Limited habitat due to wetland drainage for irrigation

The shoebill stork is also known as the whale-headed stork because of its oddly shaped bill. The species stands about 4 feet (1.22 m) tall. Its 8-inch (20.32 cm) beak is almost as wide as it is long. The young shoebill hatches from an egg the size of a baseball. The baby is fed partially chewed fish by the parents for a few weeks until it can catch insects and small fish on its own. Shoebill storks build nests on matted reeds in the swamps of east Africa.

The shoebill stork is a very large, slow-moving bird and is usually found alone or in pairs. Its bill is an adaptation that helps it feed on its favorite foods—lungfish, frogs, young turtles, and even small mammals and birds. When feeding, it stands with its bill pointed down; its neck and wings outstretched. Then it hurls itself downward and grabs its prey, parting thick vegetation with its bill. The prey is ground up by a scissoring action of the jaws, and any vegetation that was picked up is spit out.

Shoebills have huge feet—the largest feet of any of the 9,000 species of birds—built for walking on the matted reeds of their swampy home. Long toes carry the bird's weight evenly as it plods through the wetlands, searching for fish and other treats.

Like many large birds that need special habitats, the shoebill stork is in trouble. Drainage of wetlands and disturbance by cattle and people have caused its numbers to decrease drastically. It is thought that only 1,000 to 2,000 birds still remain in the African wild.

# Siamang Gibbon

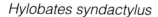

*Hylobates syndactylus*

**Range:** Malay Peninsula, Sumatra
**Habitat:** Jungle canopy, rarely on ground
**Reproduction:** Gestation: 230–235 days; 1 offspring every 2–3 years
**Size at Birth:** 1.25 lbs (.57 kg)
**Size of Adult:** 25 lbs (11.34 kg); 4 ft (1.22 m) long
**Maturation Period:** 6 years
**Diet:** Fruits (figs, grapes, and mangoes), leaves, insects, eggs, and occasionally birds
**Longevity:** 35–45 years
**Threats:** Habitat loss

Siamangs are the largest of the 6 species of gibbons, or "lesser apes," and, like all apes, they take a long time to mature. Gestation is 7 to 8 months, resulting in one baby, which stays with its mother for 2 to 3 years. During that period, the mother does not mate again. Baby siamangs, like many primates, cling to their mother's fur and travel with her nearly everywhere she goes for their first few months. The young are not sexually mature, or able to mate, until 6 years old.

Gibbons are noted for their loud calls, and are among the loudest of all mammals. The siamang emits sharp, whooping "barks" that are amplified by an inflatable throat sac in the same way that a tree frog's call is amplified. The siamang's vocal sac may be larger than its head. A group of gibbons calling wildly can be heard 2 miles away.

Gibbons are among the most amazing tree climbers in the world. The siamangs' armspan of between 5 and 6 feet (1.52–1.82 m), and their long fingers and thumbs, enable them to swing and climb for hours through the trees. This acrobatic agility also allows them to be so vocal. Most mammals would end up as another creature's dinner if they announced their presence so boldly. But gibbons "fly" through the treetops so quickly that few predators would even try to keep up.

Like human beings, siamangs will eat the food that is available. They mainly eat fruits, including figs and mangos, but also dine regularly on leaves, insects, bird eggs, and small vertebrates.

# Spectacled Bear

*Tremarctos ornatus*

**Range:** South America (Andes, from Venezuela to Bolivia)
**Habitat:** Humid forests in the foothills of the Andes, grasslands above 10,500 ft (3,200.40 m), lower lying scrub deserts
**Reproduction:** Gestation: 240–255 days; 1–3 (usually 2) cubs per season
**Size at Birth:** 11–12 lbs (4.99–5.45 kg)
**Size of Adult:** Males: 290–445 lbs (131.54–201.85 kg), 5–6 ft (1.52–1.82 m) long with a small tail of 2–3 in (5.08–7.62 cm), 36 in (91.44 cm) wide at the shoulder; Females: smaller, 175–200 lbs (79.38–90.72 kg)
**Maturation Period:** Males: 7 years; Females: 5–6 years
**Diet:** Leaves, fruits, and roots; less often insects, carrion, and young deer
**Longevity:** 20–25 years in captivity; unknown in wild
**Threats:** Human encroachment, overhunting

Bears have small babies. Young spectacled bears weigh only about half a pound (.23 kg) at birth. Even the giant polar bear gives birth to 1-pound (.45 kg) offspring. Scientists think this is because bears are such large predators that their young are relatively safe from attack. Also, female bears provide intense parental care. Typically bears give birth, and then remain isolated in a "den" for months, nursing their young until they are large enough to walk. Young spectacled bears remain with their mother for about a year before they separate and establish their own territory.

Spectacled bears are named for the light-colored rings around their eyes that sometimes resemble eyeglasses. The rest of the bear's coat is black and somewhat shaggy. Adult spectacled bears weigh from 175 to 275 pounds (79.38–124.74 kg) and stand about 3 feet (.91 m) at the shoulder when on all fours.

The spectacled bear is the only bear species native to South America. Today they are found mostly in the Andes Mountains, from Venezuela to Chile, and sometimes in Colombia and Bolivia. Small populations can be found from the coastal deserts at 600 feet (182.88 m) above sea level, all the way up to the snow line at 13,800 feet (4,206.24 m).

The major problem affecting the spectacled bear is loss of habitat. It is hard to estimate how many bears there are; perhaps only 2,000 remain in the wild.

# Texas Blind Salamander

*Typhlomolge rathbuni*

**Range:** Edwards Plateau, Hays County, Texas
**Habitat:** Underground water system of limestone caverns
**Reproduction:** Gestation: 30-day incubation of eggs
**Size at Birth:** Less than 0.5 in (1.27 cm)
**Size of Adult:** 5 in (12.70 cm)
**Maturation Period:** 5 years
**Diet:** Small aquatic invertebrates
**Longevity:** Up to 15 years
**Threats:** Groundwater pollutants

Some endangered species seem stranger than others. The Texas blind salamander is so unusual and so rare that scientists don't know much about the species.

This sightless, aquatic, cave-dwelling salamander spends its entire life underwater in limestone caverns of the Edwards Plateau in Hays County, Texas. This is the only known wild population of the Texas blind salamander.

Adult Texas blind salamanders are about 5 inches (12.70 cm) long, but the eggs laid in the water by the female are nearly microscopic. The photos here are some of the few ever taken of their reproduction, since the Cincinnati Zoo was the first place this species was bred in captivity. New hatchlings are one-half inch (1.27 cm) in length and resemble their parents in appearance with white, nearly translucent bodies and red external gill fringes on the sides of their necks.

Since Texas blind salamanders live their entire lives in total darkness, they lack both eyes and pigmentation. However, they are able to catch small invertebrates in their native pools. Even though they are sightless, they can detect the movements of their prey through the lateral line—a system of sensory organs in their skin.

There never were many Texas blind salamanders, but today they are threatened by changes in water quality and groundwater pollution. For a species like this—one that is so sensitive to changes in its environment—saving space for it is not enough. The contamination of the surroundings are as serious a threat as if there were no habitat left at all.

# Tomato Frog

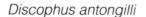

*Discophus antongilli*

**Range:** Madagascar
**Habitat:** Ponds in tropical forest
**Reproduction:** Gestation: Female lays numerous eggs and male fertilizes them externally. Tadpoles hatch from eggs and eventually metamorphose into frogs.
**Size at Birth:** Tadpole: less than 0.5 oz (14.18 g)
**Size of Adult:** 7 inches (17.78 cm) long, 5 inches (12.70 cm) wide
**Maturation Period:** 5 years
**Diet:** Insects
**Longevity:** 10–15 years
**Threats:** Habitat destruction; pollution (acid rain)

Baby frogs are called tadpoles, which in the early stages don't look at all like their parents. Tadpoles live entirely in the water and are well adapted for swimming. Adult frogs spend much of their lives on the shore. Animals that live first in water—where they hatch from eggs—and then on land are called amphibians, from Greek words that mean "double life."

The tomato frog, found only on Madagascar, gets its name from its bright red color. It digs into the dirt to find shelter and protection. Today it is endangered by severe habitat destruction. Its numbers were also decreased by the international pet trade, which took frogs from the wild until protective measures were passed. Fortunately, tomato frogs are now captively bred to supply the pet trade. Like most breeding programs, this saves frogs by preserving wild populations, and also gets people involved in local conservation.

Frogs have very sensitive skin. They actually breathe through it, and the skin is kept moist by many small mucus-secreting glands. The skin also helps maintain the water and chemical balance of the frog's body. As a result, frogs are very sensitive to pollution and are considered "indicator species," warning us to pay more attention to what we dump into the air and water.

Recent studies show that because of pollution, such as acid rain, frogs and other animals that live in bodies of water are not as abundant as they were just a few years ago.

# Zebra Duiker

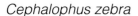

*Cephalophus zebra*

**Range:** Africa south of the Sahara
**Habitat:** Dense, lowland forest
**Reproduction:** Gestation: 6 months; 1 offspring per year
**Size at Birth:** Approx. 1–2 lbs (.45–.91 kg) at birth
**Size of Adult:** 15–25 lbs (6.81–11.34 kg); 3 ft (.91 m)
head-body length
**Maturation Period:** 1.5 years
**Diet:** Grass, leaves, roots, fruits, insects, carrion
**Longevity:** 10–15 years in captivity
**Threats:** Hunters, habitat loss

Native to the lowland forests of West Africa, from eastern Sierra Leone to the central Ivory Coast, the zebra duiker, or banded duiker, is among the smallest antelopes in the world. Duikers are similar in appearance and habits to the primitive horned ungulates that evolved during the Age of Mammals, from about 65 million to 1 million years ago.

In Africa, duikers are preyed upon by leopards, civets, small cats, and pythons. Young duikers are an easy target, so duiker mothers keep their offspring close by their sides for the first few months as they graze on the low-growing forest plants. While many of the duikers manage to survive, some are eaten. Death by predation is an integral part of life in the wild.

Local human hunters prize the duiker's flesh, and it is one of the most popular "bush meats" in West Africa. Duiker and other wild animal meat is also cheaper in village markets than the domestically ranched beef or mutton.

In Liberian traditions, the number of zebra duikers that hunters can take in their lifetimes is limited to the number of stripes on the first animal they kill. Today, though, with modern weapons, the annual kill per hunter may be dozens of duikers. But hunting is not the principal reason the zebra duiker is in danger of extinction. Their forest home is being cleared by logging and agriculture, leaving them no place to hide.

Among the world's threatened species are these beautiful animals: (clockwise from top left) cheetah, clouded leopard, American alligator, Mhorr's gazelle, (facing page, clockwise from top left) gray bat, Asian elephant, and radiated tortoise.

Lowland Gorilla

Shoebill Stork

Indian Rhinoceros

Fishing Cat

Reticulated Python

Banded Linsang

Guam Rail

Birdwing Butterfly

Siamang Gibbon

Giant Eland

Bongo Antelope

Colobus Monkey

Radiated Tortoise

Tomato Frog